This One's for You

Eleni Sophia

Dear Sam,
I hope you
enjoy the
read!
Love,
Sophia
xx

Also by Eleni Sophia (Kaur)
'Good Morning to Goodnight'

DEDICATION

I dedicate this to you
This is your sign for new beginnings
This is your reminder of how special you are
I welcome you on this journey with me

I wrote this for you
For you to find solace in my words
For you to find comfort
For you to realize your potential
For you to remember how much power you hold within you

May you keep rising
May you find your next love within yourself
May you find a home within yourself
May you reach such a level of self-love and awareness of your
worth
That no matter what anybody says or does,
You will no longer fear even the thought of having to stand alone;
May you enjoy your encounter and journey with this book,
After all,

This One's for You

Love Always,

Eleni Sophia

CONTENTS

That girl whose love was taken for granted is now doing
big things
She finds excitement in empowering fellow women
She knows how to lead
She finds joy in seeing others succeed
She is different now
She is unapologetically herself
Doing whatever in her power to make the world a better
place
She has work to do
After all, big things await her.

I wrote this for you.
I want my words to be like a warm mug of hot cocoa for
when your body aches
For when you're feeling lost
I wish for you to find solace in these words
for them to warm your soul
you are such a magnificent entity in this world

Never forget that

This One's for You

Welcome,
I welcome you exactly as you are
make yourself at home
and embark upon this journey with an open mind
I tried to craft this as carefully as possible;
Having the interior pages a warm cream to make you feel more
at home
Leaving enough space for you also to communicate your
thoughts.

May your journey be a beautiful one

The Re-direction

I title this 'The Re-direction' because bigger things await you. You may have been hurt, you may have suffered, but now, this is your opportunity to become a better version of yourself, for yourself.

Sometimes we meet people who don't treat us the way we deserve to be treated. They don't give us the respect we deserve, and it sucks. It hurts. It's so incredibly painful. And I am so sorry if you have ever spent a moment in this beautiful thing called life, questioning your worth. But this is not a loss; It is merely a re-direction.

Life has an incredible way of doing things.
An interesting way of putting us in our lowest of situations so
we can notice the beauty of the world.
So we have a chance of finding ourselves
The darkness, the seclusion, the heartache
It changes you
It leaves you questioning 'why me.'
Helpless/ curtains undrawn for days
I've been in this exact place.
The bed hasn't been freshly made in what? Around five days?
And that's okay. This is your time to grieve; dedicate this time
to treating yourself,
you deserve it.
Indulge in your favorite foods more often;
you deserve it.
 you will most definitely see the breakthrough soon.
But in actuality, all of this,
it changes you.
It opens the door for new beginnings
It transforms you into the incredible person you were always
destined to be

Years later, you learn no longer to ask, 'why me'
instead, 'what can I learn from this?'

Even more years later, you find yourself saying,
'that's why.'

Three years ago, I had so much love surging from within.
So much love I wanted to give to another, but I realized I could not provide enough- no matter how much I tried, no matter how much effort I was putting in- even if I gave it my all; simply because my cup was not full itself.

I never actually realized how many of you needed Good Morning to Goodnight as much as I did. But this is life- we struggle, we learn, we create art, and we teach.

I was giving so much, but barely anything was being reciprocated, hence the heartbreak and the publication of Good Morning to Goodnight.

In Sanskrit, 'Kaur' translates to 'princess' and is a commonly known Sikh name. Eleni is a name that I adore, and Sophia is my name. I decided to publish under this pseudonym because I was in a vulnerable state. I incorporated the name Kaur onto Eleni, yet I wanted a part of myself attached- hence the middle name. However, since Kaur has connotations with the past and this is a journey of new beginnings, I choose
Eleni Sophia.

They say you have not experienced actual pain until you have physically sat down, spoken to God and begged him to heal your heart. Three years later, I write this, thankfully and eternally gratefully,
healed.

Heartbreak taught me many things, but most importantly,
I learned how to be patient.
My relationship with the divine is stronger than it has ever
been-
I discovered no matter who leaves,
if I have myself and God
I will forever be okay

Heartbreak taught me to fall in love with the one person that
will forever remain
The one person who will hold me down the most-
Myself.
I can guarantee you, as soon as you realize you are the only
person that can save yourself, your outlook on life changes.

The infinite power you hold within you
Cherish that
Unleash it.

Heartbreak,
It built me,
changed me and
Ultimately,
it was the catalyst to opening a door for me to embark upon a
new beautiful path of my journey.

Three years later, I rise, stronger than ever and to prove to you,
healing is possible.
You will get through whatever life throws at you because
everything happens for your growth and your betterment.

That heartache was an opportunity for me to learn what I want
from this world
I had to find myself; I had an urgency to do so.
I was continually trying to give, give, give
but I learned, how could I possibly try and
give
from a cup that wasn't even full itself

And that is when I realized
It is not love that is bad
It is not love at all
Nor was I the 'problem.'
It simply was not the right person for me
an incredible thing heartbreak taught me;
the importance of self-love
my darling, fill your cup with endless self-love
Let self-love consume you entirely
Let self-love be oxytocin to your body
and
Let it captivate your bones with self-acceptance

And I know these words alone are not enough; they help for a while and wear off. However, I invite you to make yourself so comfortable that you can welcome yourself back at any time to find solace in these words. Write your poetry all over these pages; scribble how you feel, draw, and create your art- find your catharsis;
I pray you do.

Take a deep breath, wherever you are and remind yourself,
You are so incredibly special
You have the whole universe within you
Your love may have been taken for granted
But this is not a reflection of you.

Take a deep breath and remind yourself
Remind yourself of how powerful you are
How your pure heart contains nothing but good intentions.
Remind yourself
You gave someone your love
You put their happiness before your own
But all this means that you can love and that is so incredibly
special.
Remind yourself
The sooner you let go, the more room you are making for
beautiful occurrences to enter your life

And with a heart like yours,
No, you did not deserve to be treated as such
But I hope you find encouragement through these words
I hope you realize everything in the cosmos is working for you
And with a hear like yours,
One day, someone will consider themselves the luckiest in the world
To be loved by
a heart like yours

The universe is always conspiring to give you exactly what you need at precisely the right time.

Continue to tell yourself that one day, everything that happens in your life will suddenly start making sense to you.

And I know things may seem harsh now
And you keep questioning yourself whether light will come

But once you start accepting what has happened and how everything happens for a reason, things will not seem so bad.

Write exactly how you feel
Express your feelings in some way or another

Days will get easier as they pass;
You will learn how to pick yourself back up and be your own best friend first, and you will manage to hold your own hand-even in the toughest of situations and that is when you will know,
you have grown.

This journey of recovery will be a lonely one
But it will be so incredibly vital and beneficial to your personal growth.
One day, you will look back and realize why you and this person crossed paths.
And I know right now the sound of this day seems so far away but once you start believing that your time is coming and reminding yourself that, each day you are getting closer and closer to reaching an incredible level of self-love,
you will be extremely motivated
you will have hope
and with hope,
we thrive

So, my darling, that loss you spend hours grieving over, in
actuality, it is your gain
Everything in this beautiful world is remarkably a blessing in
disguise;
life has an interesting way of doing things;
putting us in our worst situations
so we can blossom and bloom into the beautiful people we
were destined to be

A brand-new life awaits you
So many opportunities are waiting to be welcomed at your
door
Welcome them in
You only grow after taking yourself out of your comfort zone

My darling,
You have the whole universe within you
So whenever you feel overwhelmed
Remind yourself,
this is merely a re-direction and a lesson on how to love
yourself
Break-ups can be so incredibly lonely but once you start taking
advantage of this time alone, cherish it.
Be patient with yourself and the timing that is destined for you.
There will come a time where you decide to choose yourself,
and from that day onwards, you will become ultimately, entirely
and exclusively, unstoppable

A soul like yours
Deserves all the astonishing things that this world has to offer
and more

May you grow through this pain
May you conquer through
It sure takes its precious time
But during this time take the liberty to find yourself
This world has big plans for you
Write down your goals and start working towards them
Each day do get closer to accomplishing your goals

This world has so much in store for you
You just have to be open to receive it

Do not neglect yourself and your well-being
You are so important, complete and perfect
On your own

From pain, we must grow
Evolve
Shine
Growth is inevitably beautiful and nourishing to your soul
One day you will look back and realize why everything
collapsed; there is always beauty after chaos.

We all have our unique paths
While some of us take longer than others to heal
Everything is provided to us, for us

No matter what situation you find yourself in
When you trust and have faith
Whether this be a strong belief within yourself,
or the divine
The pace of healing will fasten

May your journey of healing be a beautiful one

For some reason, it always seems to be the purest hearts
who get broken
It is so rare to find someone with similar intentions to you
Someone whose intentions are just as pure
And sometimes it is the most purest hearts that endure the
most pain;
I know,
Your heart has been through so much,
You deserve to devote some time to yourself
Focus upon your desires and what you want
Be so unapologetically free
Liberate yourself from any vibes that make you question
your being
And when you are least expecting it
Things will start blooming
Keep going
;
Amazing things await you

It's the type of love that makes you feel all sorts of wonderful
things
It makes you feel
Worthy of everything
That love, that love is called

Self-love

And until the love you are craving reaches you
Learn to love yourself first
Every single cell in your body is fighting for you,
Learn to stand up on your own
Use this as an opportunity to open doors to big things that are
awaiting you

Take advantage of this time to fall in love with every single scar
on your body
Love will find you
But until it does
Please, take all the time you need to heal
Cherish your body
Fall in love with your scars and your imperfections
After all, it is your imperfections that make you so perfect

Crystals are most potent in their purest form
So why do you undermine yourself
Dig deeper into your true genuine, authentic self
Unleash
Show up in your purest form;

There is something so stunningly special and precious about being in your rawest form.

Stay raw and be truly authentically yourself.

I pray you find a home within yourself
You find solace in your own comfort
You cherish and fall in love with every cell of your body
May you fall in love with your insecurities;
after all, all these fragments you see as imperfections are
indeed perfection.

I pray you become exactly who you want to be
I hope you learn to take each opportunity as it comes and
Nourish each moment in your life

Find love deep within yourself
All that love you want to shower another person with
Go deep within
And shower yourself
Engulf it and consume it with pride
You deserve respect
You deserve your own love
After all, when somebody sees the way you treat yourself
They will want to up their game

Before even considering approaching you

But these experiences enter our lives as catalysts for
wonderful things to blossom
Especially when you step out of your comfort zone
When you do things that scare you
When the universe sees you releasing and trusting, it starts
manifesting pleasing things in your favor
Everything significant begins with through the beautiful art
of faith
The fascinating aspects of faith teach you that no matter
what you go through, the universe is always going to be there
It is similar to the force of gravity, its always holding you
down
Faith, faith keeps you going and helps you evolve and
liberate yourself

Faith, it is beautiful
Hold onto it

I believe we all go through things and experiences in life, so
we can grow, evolve, learn and therefore help others
This world is so magnificent, and people need someone as
significant as yourself
Create art, share it with the world
It is ultimately the living circle of humans
We experience, we create art, we heal, and we help others

This is the beginning of a new, abundant and satisfying life
But with this comes the beauty of patience
And with the virtue of patience
Comes faith.

There will be light at the end of the tunnel.

There most certainly will.

My darling, a word of advice, embrace being single
Embrace each moment of being alone
Dining alone
Do not be afraid to sit at the table alone
Own it.
Take ownership of all the beautiful things in your life
A lot of the time we are so afraid to go out or eat out alone
because we are so distracted by the opinions of others-
what others think…
Look on the positives, if people see you comfortable, eating
alone
There is a possibility of them too, being encouraged and
inspired by you

This world is so big and full of so many beautiful opportunities that
once you start believing that everything is coming together for you,
blessings will inevitably fall into place.

A beautiful journey of life starts from the simple art of faith and trust
Knowing and trusting that you will be okay
Knowing and trusting whether things are going the way you wish or differently,
In actuality,
everything is actually coming together for you.

Life is so magical
And there are so many beautiful things awaiting you;

After every fail or lesson is derived an opportunity

Everything is a lesson-
even sometimes when life feels like it
is getting 'too much.'
You are just evolving and most importantly,

You are never alone

Let the universe do its magic
Trust it;
After all, it wants the best for you

When you expect magic
Magic will express itself

All of this is temporary
Whatever you are feeling
This shall pass.
Everything is transient

I pray you remain humble during the blessings and encouraged
throughout the journey
After all,
Everything is happening for you
It is all in your favor

At the end of the day
We must fall
To rise
We must learn from our journey, and we must continue to
put ourselves first
Even if we are standing alone.

Do not worry,
After all,

A new fresh life awaits you
Everything is coming together.

This One's for You

I want to let you in on a secret;
From the moment you took your first breath
The universe was prepared and rigged to be in your favor.
it decided that once this beautiful entity
entered the world, everything in this journey of theirs
would be for their betterment;
A clear path was laid out
A clear journey with different paths depending upon
whichever
decision you embarked
The universe wants to take care of you,
You just need to trust that;
When the cosmos see you believing
They take a moment and smile;
They love a stubborn heart full of faith bigger than fear
They will fight for you

And with this mindset, you will find your treasure.

The universe will send whatever you desire,
When you are ready to receive it
If what you ask for does not reach you
Know, much better things are making their way towards
you.

Believe me when I say
when your faith is strong
No matter who goes against you
As long as you keep your head held high and your faith
strong
You will be at your happiest

And never give up because the universe loves a stubborn
heart;
It shows you trust it more
The galaxies adore those who believe in them

Beautiful things blossom in their own timing and
The universe loves and cherishes a soul who trusts it
The one that steps out of their comfort zone
Living life unapologetically
Giving back and serving to those who may need some love-
even from a warm smile
The universe will reward you
It sees you
It is proud of you.

Each time I get nervous, I take a deep breath and hear the voice
inside my head say, 'You have the entire universe within you.'
It is from that moment;
I remind myself
The universe is on my side, it always has been, and it always
will
Everything comes with trust

The next stages of your life will require a lot of discipline, patience, fantastic energy, and strong faith because, with all these ingredients, you begin to rise gracefully.

I wrote this for you.
An incredible human being with so much potential within
Deserves to remember why they are here
&
Deserves to remember exactly who they are

My darling, you do not need saving. You just need to re-align within yourself and go deep within to find out who you really are and what you want from this world.

For you to notice the light after the dark
For you to see the beautiful growth potential after pain
For you to notice that there is nothing wrong with being re-directed when things don't go as planned

May you continue to evolve steadily

And yes, upon this journey people will question you
There will be people who do not believe in you
But when your faith outweighs not only your fears but the
opinions of others
You will have such a beautiful journey and a fantastic story
to tell.

Oceans beneath us
The planets above us
Us, in between
Don't ever think you are not a miracle
When God created you, he knew the world needed a you

I believe all humans are interconnected; after all, we are all derived from the same divine source.

We all cross each other's paths for a reason; whether they come into our lives to complement ours, whether we evolve together or whether they come here to help us

Some may disconnect from us through our journeys, and I know it can seem daunting and scary, but at the same time, they departed at the universe's divine timing.

I know it is difficult to comprehend, but I promise you, one day, you will look back and everything, every little piece will look like a completed puzzle.

And ironically, the situation will be puzzle-less.
It will be clear.

Please do not spend time finding validation through others
You are so incredible and hold so much potential within
Once you believe in yourself
You will be unstoppable

As long as you have yourself
As long as you remember to and forever promise to
Never lose yourself again,

                                    You will be okay

May you be fearless,
brave
Faithful to yourself
Be light wherever you go
Be happy for others and remember
Your time is coming

;

One day you will have it all
Everything will come together
But all of this comes with trust and belief
Faith within the universe that you are being taken care of
That you are being guided

I wrote this for you because you are worth so much
I wrote this to remind you of how worthy you are
To tell you to be unapologetically you

In this very precious thing called life

and there will be days where you feel like everything is okay
and there will be those that you will make you question
whether you will ever get through this

Don't be so hard on yourself and take each day as it comes
Let out your emotions;
Write, draw, cry, pray and release all your resistance
Liberate yourself

Once you get used to your own company,
You start to realize you are the only person you ever need
Yes, people come into our lives to complement ours
But in the end, we are all we have

We are such significant beings in this divine universe
If we don't even dare to love ourselves,
We cannot expect to be embraced in the way that we do

Soon,

Nobody else's opinions will matter
You will be standing so firm on your ground
That no matter what comes your way, you will conquer

Some days things may seem harsh, and that is okay
You do not need to have everything sorted out
Some days you will do really well in terms of not thinking
about this person
And maybe the day after suddenly you have a random wave
of missing them
I know how this feels
I've been there.
And these feelings are okay

And it does not matter if you have no bright outlook on
where this is going because incredible things are unfolding
for you
Because even if you hold a teaspoon of faith

You will be okay

I am so incredibly sorry somebody made you feel as though it was difficult to love you
I am so incredibly sorry if you have ever felt this way.
But I promise you, the universe will send you someone so unexpectedly. Someone that will every day and forever remind you of how great you are. Someone who will reinforce your belief in love as well as in yourself. Someone who will see your flaws but will forever remind you that your imperfections are what make you so perfect. Just tightly hold onto this belief.
In the meantime, fall in love with yourself- fall in love with your own company, cherish your body and scars before anybody else can and

One day, you will see it all

Even Oprah says that,
The only difference between a celebrity and an ordinary person is that
the celebrity is known to more people.
When we start to realize this, we eradicate the pedestals we have
created in our minds
When we remember that we are all the same;
We are all derived from the same source,
We all have the exact same capabilities within us just as much as
anyone else-
We wholly and slowly eliminate the destructing nature of comparison
And consequently,
We find ourselves chasing our dreams
And living a much healthier and abundant life
than ever before

May your heart find someone deserving of cherishing it.
There will always be people that want you
But there will be the one genuine person out there that
genuinely deserves having you

Choose who gets to find a home within your heart,
wisely

Wish them the very best
And let them walk away
If they don't want to be a part of your life anymore
Maybe its time for this particular journey to end.

And I know it's hard
It is so incredibly hard;
You're left wondering what you did wrong
But I urge you to shift your perspective;
If you can give so much compassion to the wrong one
Think about how much you will be able to give to the one
meant for you.
The fact that you were able to show so much emotion
shows how much you can love, and that is truly magnificent.

Maybe one day you will cross paths
Grown and evolved
You will look back with clarity
And realize why things happened

If they are meant to be in your life
Inevitably,
It will happen.

For now,
Continue to put yourself first
It's finally time to start making yourself a priority
Putting your happiness first
You deserve everything this world has to offer and more
Learn to give it to yourself first

You will see why.

One day the welcome mat at your door will be full of imperfectly perfect muddy prints all of different sizes

And that will make your house a home

The imprints of tiny footsteps
The love within the home
The crusts from toast lying on the kitchen tabletop
The sound of a baby or two
Hearing 'honey I'm home.'
Toys all over the playroom
Waking up next to him beside you, smiling- (inevitably)

That will make your house a home.

and you will take an exhilarating breath
Eyes closed
Goosebumps.
And you will take a moment of reflection and thank God for everything in your life

For making you wait.

Your time is coming
It is making its way to you
It will all be worth every second you waited.

And my goodness, will you be so thankful it didn't work with another.

Never lose hope;
this is everything you have ever wanted.

if not, it is unquestionably more.

A Woman like Her

She was beautiful, but it was her heart and soul that
captivated the lives of many.

Her inner beauty complemented her outer beauty to such an
extent that people always remembered the effects they had
upon having the privilege of even meeting a woman like her

She walks in deep faith
And that is what makes her so fearless
Her heart is guarded with self-love
But is open to blessings
Full of wisdom and drowned in faith
How could one forget a woman like her?

A woman like you is worth so much more than the ordinary
You deserve endless amounts of love and salvation
With every breath, flowers grow from within your lungs
Never forget how irresistible you are

In a world of chaos
She will be your solace
Your comfort
Your right hand
Your shoulder when you need one
Your rock
When the world doesn't seem so friendly anymore,
She will be your go-to
It is her presence that you will crave

She knows that men too deserve to be treated with respect
Just as much as her
They also deserve to be called handsome and to be spoiled
She knows the importance of showering her future husband
and kids in prayer

She understands that the same go for our men too
She knows that good men still exist

She knows the importance of showering him with love too
Just as much as she desires to be cherished herself.

She knows to appreciate him just as much as he cherishes
her
After all,
Our men deserve love too
They too deserve to be told how well they are doing and
how proud we are of them

They deserve to be told how much we appreciate their efforts
and how much they do for us.

Just as much as we do

She may be young, but she sees beyond life
Her experiences shape her, and her perspective is different;
She learns from the lessons and takes her 'failures' as opportunities
She lives life on her own terms but yet she remains grounded

She's the type of woman that can stand firmly on her own ground, yet she knows when to draw the line and maintain respect.

She expects nothing from nobody;
She is the independent, ambitious, focused queen people look up to
She spreads her energy wisely
Spreads her love accordingly

With the love she has to give
You will be enticed from her soul alone

There is life before her
And life after her
You will be enticed through her greatness

She fell in love with her own company and cherished it
wisely.
To them it was loneliness
But she knew, she knew it was the best form of
liberty

Nobody has anything on her
And I'm not even talking about looks
The way her soul captivates minds
The way she leaves people feeling
She is herself
Unapologetically herself*
And that is her superpower
Doing what she does best and continues to thrive
                                        She stops for nobody

And when after realizing her worth
She chooses you
You too must remember and recognize that you must be an
incredible human being for her to want you- to be so lucky to
have someone like her

She is a luxury- not for everybody
Just the one who sees her value
The one who respects her
And until he comes
She will continue to shower herself with all the love she
deserves
So she too can protect his heart

In such a corrupt, mundane world, she is luxury

It is her delicate touch
Softness
In control
Knows how to handle a situation
She's the bravest and courageous of them all
With all that ambition building within her
With all that compassion bursting from within her
                She embraces the glorious woman from within

With a heart like hers
You will never want to let her go
You would never even consider letting her go

To My Beautiful, Powerful Women,

Our bodies hold such significant power
Such beauty;
New lives are conceived within our bodies
We bring life into this world

We hold the strength and beauty to do this
I pray you are never left questioning your capabilities
I pray you are never left feeling insecure about the shape of
your body
I pray you fall in love with your scars for they all hold a story
behind them
I pray you realize, the way your body is shaped will one day,
protect and be a home for your little one

After all, you are such a significant entity in this world
Do not let anybody treat you any different

With a lady like her by your side
You will feel on top of the world
Constantly exhilarated by her aura
Eager to hear her softly spoken words
Yet mind-blowing thoughts
She is the balance you need

She has mastered the beauty of being the epitome of soft
yet strong
Soft- able to love and ready to receive love
Powerful- possessing the strength to leave the table
when respect is no longer being served

She knows her worth

After all, she is a goddess

As you get to know her
Each layer will be shiner and spark more ...
Each layer will be more beautiful than the previous.

Until you reach her inside
Her heart
That's when you've found her treasure

Beautiful than ever

;

Courageousness and softness, encompassed within one
individual
The beauty of her heart and mind will forever outweigh that
of her exterior

And when a love like hers arrives
Hold her with delicacy but do not leash onto her
Let her be the free spirit she is
Exploring the beauty of the world
Yet
Loving you so exclusively
Make sure to treat it with gentle care

She's the type of woman you will regret not fighting for
After all, with a woman like her by your side,
You will feel as if anything is possible.
She will unleash the king from within you
She has such a strong desire to help you manifest your
visions just as much as her own
She has a burning desire to stay by your side- yes, even when
you have nothing.
You will regret not keeping her

Some women are once in a lifetime
She. Is. That. Woman.

A woman that wants you to be successful
The one that will invest in her own vision as well as yours
The type of woman that will encourage and captivate you

Still, maintaining an overflowing of self-love and self-respect
That when respect is no longer being served
She will happily sit on the table alone

Her intentions are purer than that of a first love's

She is the most liberated when drowned in faith

It is her majestic raw that
She maintains within herself
Her visions are clear, and her relationship with God is
getting stronger and stronger each day

Magic lingers from her eyes
Magic articulates itself through her smile
Magic expresses itself from within her soul
And don't even get me started on how magical you feel after
having a conversation with her

Living within her
Lies ambition and endless love
However
If you have no intentions of keeping her

                                                    Set her free

She understands the importance of prayer and showering
her loved ones alongside the almighty
It is her strong faith that takes her to unimaginable places
Her mindset
Her connection with the universe
Her strong relationship with the most high

With all the compassion in her heart,
she deserves nothing but pure love

souls like hers are so incredibly rare
;
She is a rarity in this world

She will transform your weaknesses into strengths
And with her by your side, you will feel on top of the world;
Her prayers will move all obstacles in your way
And you
Too,
will be
More liberated than ever

And even in your darkest of moments,
Even times when you no longer believe in yourself and
situations get tough,
She will be right there,
rooting for you,
Remaining right by your side.

And that, that right there is not only a good woman but one
worth cherishing your entire life

Her prayers are derived purely deep from within her, and
my goodness will they move mountains for you
She knows the importance of showering her man in as
much love and prayer as she desires for herself

And that
forever maintains one of her reflective, elegant qualities

Lust in itself maintains an expiration date
Prayer and a woman of faith
Is worth a lifetime and many more

Brave girl,
do not let this heartache discourage you,
Keep your mind open;
one day, you will put yourself in the vulnerable position of
being in love again
and
brave girl,
You will have found yourself.

Strong-minded, contentious, young woman
never forget who you are.

Brave girl,
never forget how unstoppable you are
never lower your standards.
Courageous girl, never think you are asking for 'too much.'
;
If he is the one
He will do everything in his right mind to protect and fight
for you

Beautiful girl
With everything going for her,
Do not let the opinions of others stop you
Do not stop until you are satisfied

Know your worth,
Please do not let anybody mistreat you- whether that be a friend or a 'lover'
Find yourself- glorify your body, fall in love with your scars, accept your flaws, and most of all, do not forget who you are.
You are amazing, you are powerful, and you deserve the world and more

And the one lucky enough to cherish her heart
is the one who considers himself
The luckiest man to ever set foot on this earth

With so much going for her
Balancing the two most robust relationships in her life;
Her relationship with God and the one with herself
Carrying so much
Learning each day

'How does she do it?' They ask

The ferocity she carries with her,
leaves them mute.

Her strength is contagious
Her ambition drives them insane

But she stops for no one

She will accomplish it all,
With or
without
a knight by her side

After all,

She is a warrior.

God Sent Love

I hope that one day you can look back and see everything
with clarity, notice precisely why things happened in the way
that they did

Love will arrive in the most unexpected way
And when it does,
You will know it is God-given
From the way that it feels,

The energy they give off
The way they are with you
The way they treat you
How at home you feel
And ultimately,
How happy you are.

And this love may take its time to arrive
In fact, let this love take its time to
arrive
;
When you are finally ready to say yes
You, yourself will know this is right.

But when it does
My goodness will it be beautiful
Because not only are you whole and complete on your own
You have proved to the universe you are ready since your cup
is now full
The universe has sent this incredible human being to you in its
divine timing.

It will be beautiful.

Do not search for your other half because my love, you are
not half
You are a whole within yourself
You are complete.

When this love arrives,
In his mind, it will be both of you
against the world.

If he is sane
He will do anything and everything in his right mind to
fight for you
And to keep you happy-
Anything in his power to keep fighting for you- he
won't second guess it
;
He'll just do it

Do not settle until this individual has found his way to you

And when this God-sent love arrives
You will be over the moon that it did not work out with anybody else
Now, you will physically be thanking God every day for intertwining paths with this individual. You will thank him for healing your heart, and you will be so incredibly appreciative for the way things have happened.

You will have this exhilarating feeling of liberation
The past is behind
Your paths have intertwined for something beautiful to
blossom
Let it flow

And even when love does find you
And you are whole and complete yourself
You might still be in a vulnerable position
But you will know you are so secure on your own
As long as you do not lose yourself again
Everything will be okay

And I know when love arrives after heartbreak, you put yourself in a vulnerable position- the possibility of being hurt But that rollercoaster ride that you have just completed is the epitome of everything happening in your favor. It has taught you many life experiences.

You are in the position of the highest form of self-love, that you have learned to leave the table when respect is no longer being served.
There is no fear of dining alone
You have conquered and may you continue to conquer

And it is perfectly okay to be vulnerable- just trust that beautiful things are on their way, and I guarantee you, with this open mindset, you will continue to live an all-embracing life.

And together, you will be unstoppable

This love will never leave you fighting alone
From the start
It will feel like a team
Support on support
Building individual empires then coming along and outshining
together
You deserved more than what you previously had
I hope you realize that
I hope you realize how much you deserve from this world
there is a man out there willing to fight for you
Don't give up until that love finds you
But first, don't forget to find yourself.
Take advantage of this time alone.

Be courageous enough to find yourself
Brave enough to fill your cup alone

And sometimes you and love may have disagreements
And that is beautiful.
You are not afraid to say your opinion, and that shows how
comfortable you are
Yes, having disagreements and compromising and building
together
It is beautiful.
During these disagreements, remind yourselves it is never you
two against each other;
You are a team
It is you both against the problem.

Love will fight for you in the toughest of situations
Love, love will never give up on you

My goodness are they right when they say this love finds
you blindly
When you're least expecting it
When you're focused, and the universe is a witness to your
readiness upon this new journey

The kind of love where you both find yourselves remembering
the days you prayed for something like this

That love is worth cherishing

And my darling, when this arrives, you will know this is what
love is supposed to feel like
You will feel it deep in your bones
It will feel so effortless
It will be so effortless
It will naturally flow
And you will be so thankful
This love will manifest into something incredible

And when you welcome this love
If this love brings you peace
When you're not left questioning where you stand
When you're secure
When it feels so incredibly natural- as though the universe is
bringing you together
The one that feels like magic,
That's it.
That's the one

A relationship where respect is reciprocated
A Godly relationship where you pray together
repent together
Encourage each other
Support one another
They exist.

Yes, they are rare
But they still exist
When you pray for what you want,
When the Most High knows you are
ready
You shall receive

;

You always receive.

And even when love does find you
And even when you are whole and complete yourself
There might be times where you are vulnerable
And that is okay.
You have been hurt, but you are giving love another go, and
my goodness does that make you brave?!

Just remind yourself of how far you have come;
You should be so incredibly proud of yourself
And most importantly, when you remind yourself that you
are whole and complete on your own,
As long as you do not lose yourself again
Everything will be completely fine.

And remember,
He chose you
As much as you chose you,
so did he.
This is a new journey, the previous door has closed, and you
are embarking upon a fresh, beautiful journey with an
incredible individual;
Just because another didn't appreciate you for who you are- life
will not repeat itself
Things have changed now.

The kind of love where you both find yourselves
reminiscing
over the days you prayed for something like this
and ask yourselves,

How could we have possibly loved each other,
If our cups weren't even full when we were alone?

We outgrew our own weaknesses alone and came together
in
strength and prayer

You are both rarities in this world and deserve one other

In a world where
Loyalty is deployed a luxury
Where commitment is so rare,
Compromise is key.

We live in a society where our egos consume us
many of us are so self-indulged and continuously focus on what
we want- forgetting our partners' desires
But
Once we put these aside and learn to compromise

We will have the strength to communicate better
Grow and evolve together
And of course, this will have to be two-sided for something beautiful to flourish

and if it is true love,
Both sides will compromise for one another and fight for each other

I can tell you now
With faith and with self-love,
Learning how to compromise
You will find love

And
There will be no expiration date

You deserve somebody unafraid to communicate their
feelings
Somebody mature enough to tell you how they feel

If two people want to make it work
They will fight to be together
They will go against all odds

Do not settle until you find someone unafraid to go to the
ends
of the world for you

After all, my love,
You deserve it all

I wrote this to reassure you that good experiences are on their way. I wrote this to remind you to never give up on love; You might be suffering right now, but I guarantee you, in a few months, you will see exactly why things happened in the way that
they did.

The universe will always fight for souls to be together- essentially if they are written and destined to be together, nothing can stop them from being apart. Remember, from the moment you entered into this world, the universe was rigged; everything was crafted individually in your favor- a beautiful journey awaits you- with faith and trust, I pray you are healed most divinely. I pray you complete yourself with such intense self-love that you are your own dose of oxytocin and may you experience the most striking feeling of love, you have ever felt.

I pray your level of self-love is so high that when somebody mistreats you or if they are willing to leave, you no longer beg them to stay; you will happily open the door. After all, anything that is holding you back from your purpose ultimately does not belong in your life. I pray you prove and demonstrate to those who ever doubted you wrong that you can achieve success no matter what; never forget how worthy and powerful you are. I wrote this for you, for all the incredible souls striving to be better versions of themselves, doing things each day to get closer to their goals. For all of you with a different perspective on life, your time is coming- whether this is in terms of love or success, your time is coming; everything is happening in divine timing.

You might have already reached your stage of healing and learned so much. You should be so proud of how far you have
come
;
within those scars and through those obstacles
You discovered how to heal and love alone, and that is beautiful.

Courageousness and softness are encompassed within
one individual; you are the balance that this world needs;
The beauty of your heart and mind will forever outweigh that of your exterior, and I pray you never forget how important you are.

The universe loves a stubborn heart,
especially when you never give up on your dreams
and you trust, when you are free,
When it sees you full of faith and compassion,
It will do everything in its power to provide for you
Its magic will shine all over you.

One day, your love will be appreciated to such an extent that everything will be peaceful; your intertwined journeys will be like a flowing river, manifesting beautiful things along the way. And of course, there will be bumps but how you manage to find your way through maturely is what matters; this love will be so real and genuine, you won't be left fighting for attention.

It will flow so beautifully and my goodness, will you be so grateful it didn't work out with what you once thought you wanted.

About the Publisher

Founded by Sophia, herself, Perspective Press Global is a
publishing house specializing in works of motivation and
poetry.

When Sophia was thirteen years old, she had completed
a novella but because she was 'too young,'
she was consequently faced with
rejection.

It was never to do with the quality of her work, instead
because most publishing houses published those
over the age of twenty.

Sophia then decided to go down the route
of self-publishing, and her books were such a success
that her quotes were reaching thousands across the globe!

At Perspective Press Global, our mission is to inspire
young aspiring authors that there is no such thing as being
'too young;' your voices deserve to be heard.

At Perspective Press Global, we see your potential;
ultimately, you are the next generation.

For submissions, please visit our website

Perspectivepressglobal.com

Also by Eleni Sophia-

Poetry collection, 'Good Morning to Goodnight' about love and heartbreak.

And 'Perspective by Sophia'- a motivational book, where Sophia simplifies the 'law of attraction' and encourages you on living a life that you love, just by changing your mindsets!

Signed copies of all books can be found on

Perspectivepressglobal.com

46534978R00063

Printed in Poland
by Amazon Fulfillment
Poland Sp. z o.o., Wrocław